GARDENS OF EUROPE

A Pictorial Tour

GARDENS OF EUROPE

A Pictorial Tour

with descriptions and directions for visiting them

Text by Dorothy Loa McFadden

Pictures by James L. and Dorothy Loa McFadden

South Brunswick and New York: *A. S. Barnes and Company*
London: *Thomas Yoseloff Ltd*

A. S. Barnes and Co., Inc.
Cranbury, New Jersey 08512

Thomas Yoseloff Ltd
108 New Bond Street
London W1Y OQX, England

SBN 498 07576 1
Printed in the United States of America

To the wonderful joyous members
of The Home Garden Club of Morristown, N.J.

CONTENTS

*Numbers followed by "C" refer to photographs in color.

PREFACE

GARDEN PHOTOGRAPHY IS OUR HOBBY

For the last ten years, when my husband and I were on extensive business trips in Europe, we spent weekends visiting gardens open to the public and photographing them—he with his Voigtlaender Bessamatic, and Rolleiflex, I with my Retina Kodak IV. We were fascinated with their great variety, the interesting details, the features characteristic of landscape design in different countries. We concentrated on formal or flower gardens, rather than on the "English Gardens" —which we in America would call landscaped parks—because of our love of colorful bloom and design.

We found so little information available in each country as to where the best gardens were located, what their special attractions were, and when they were open, that I felt compelled to write a book including all this information for other garden-loving travelers. *Touring the Gardens of Europe,* published by McKay, was the result. It includes very detailed descriptions of some of the gardens shown in the present book. In addition, it has a guide to over 800 gardens in 18 countries, with "Circle Tour" maps showing gardens within a 30-mile radius of central points.

This first book, however, had only 12 monochrome illustrations, and people who saw my color slide lectures on European gardens often asked me, "Why don't you do a book of your pictures?" So here it is.

The present book is arranged deliberately by types of gardens and their details, rather than by countries, as I hoped it would give ideas to many home gardeners. The descriptions of the gardens, however, are arranged by countries for use by travelers, and include information on hours when they are open and how to reach them.

ACKNOWLEDGMENTS

We are very grateful to the many owners of private gardens who so generously open them to the public; to our friend Anne M. Hatcher, APSA, for her expert advice in choosing the illustrations; and to Dr. Walter D. Paist, whose painstaking skill made possible the transformation of many of our color slides into black and white pictures.

GARDENS OF EUROPE

A Pictorial Tour

1

DESCRIPTIONS OF GARDENS
AND DIRECTIONS FOR VISITING THEM

The following descriptions of the gardens pictured in this book are arranged alphabetically and by countries. Hours of admission are given—as well as location—but it would be advisable to check in advance when in the neighborhood, for hours are sometimes changed.

For Great Britain and Northern Ireland, the booklet published annually called "Historic Houses, Castles and Gardens" is invaluable, as it gives the up-to-date hours when open, also road and bus directions. It is obtainable for $1.00 from the British Book Centre, 996 Lexington Ave., New York, N. Y. 10017.

Where the initials "G.S." or "S.G.S." follow the garden description, this means they may be visited on special days for charity, arranged for by: the Gardens Scheme of England and Wales, 57 Lower Belgrave St., London S.W.1, England (the price of the booklet, available annually in April and giving opening days, is 3s [50¢ including postage]); and Scotland's Garden Scheme, 26 Castle Terrace, Edinburgh 1, Scotland, price 2/6 (50¢ including postage). Many estate owners open their beautiful homes and gardens in this way.

The initials "N.T." stand for National Trust property. A membership contribution not only allows one free access to these gardens, but helps to preserve them. There is also a "Passport to Britain," given out by the British Travel Association anywhere outside Great Britain, for tourists who would like a season ticket to all National Trust properties as well as those owned by the Ministry of Public Buildings and Works. Admission fees to the gardens listed in this book, however, are always very small.

The numbers in parentheses refer to the pictures, those with the letter "C" being the color plates.

Denmark

Gavnø Manor, Near Naestved, Zealand, Denmark (about
48 miles south of Copenhagen) (29)

A castle estate of Baron Axel Roodt-Thott, a descendant of earlier owners.
Many rooms, a famous picture collection, and the chapel may be visited. In May
there are 100,000 spring bulbs in the 12½-acre park. Later there are annuals,
a rose garden, and herbaceous borders. The park is open daily from 10 to 8, the
castle 10 to 5, except for Friday when the gallery is closed.

Tivoli Gardens, Copenhagen, Denmark (31C, 116, 117)

A beautiful recreation park with every building and garden area done in
good taste. When lighted at night it is like fairyland. Every restaurant has its
own flower borders and fountains in an infinite variety. Open from May 1 to
mid-September, 9 to midnight.

Eire

Annesgrove, Castletownroche, County Cork, Eire
(about 30 miles north of Cork) (114)

On the upper level of these extensive gardens—where Spenser wrote his
Faerie Queene—are paths lined with choice rhododendrons and azaleas grown
from seed. There is also a lovely old-fashioned walled garden of perennials, and
a small rock garden surrounding a rustic summerhouse. Along the River Awbeg
below is another garden of water-loving plants, among them primulas, astilbes,
and ferns, with flowering Japanese cherries overhead. Telephone Mr. Annesley
for an appointment.

Garinish Island, Glengarriff, County Cork, Eire
(about 50 miles west of Cork) (24)

This is a 19-acre garden, partly formal, partly naturalized, designed in the
early 20th century by Harold Peto. The winding paths pass through many exotic
trees and shrubs, native hollies, flaming azaleas, and fine rhododendrons. All grow

to great size in this west coast climate warmed by the Gulf Stream. The formal
Italian garden is particularly beautiful in spring when the edges of the pool are
bright with forget-me-nots and azaleas. There is also a charming walled perennial
garden. Property of the Irish government, it is open daily from 10 to 5:30. To
reach the island take a small motorboat for 20 minutes from Glengarriff. Some
bus tours include this garden.

Glasnevin Botanical Gardens, Dublin, Eire (9C)

A garden of beauty as well as botanical interest. The wide perennial borders
with each plant carefully marked, the fine rock garden, the collection of ferns,
the interesting squares of weeds with which the home gardener should become
familiar, the many unusual old trees—all these and much more invite a lengthy
visit. Open weekdays from 9 to 6, Sunday 11 to 6; greenhouses weekdays 10 to 6,
Sunday 2 to 6.

Glen Veagh, Veagh, County Donegal, Eire (northwest of Letterkenny) (62)

This is an astonishingly lush garden set in the midst of vast acres of bleak
moors. There is a kitchen garden with fruit trees, a natural wildflower garden,
a small stream with flowers along its edges, and a walk with fine species of rhododendrons. Open from 3 to 5 only in May, June, and July on days when the
owner, the American Henry P. McIlhenny, is absent, so one must write or phone
the Estate Agent for an appointment.

Japanese Garden, Tully, County Kildare, Eire
(30 miles southwest of Dublin) (36, 37, 38)

Created in 1906–1910 for Lord Wavertree by his Japanese gardener Eida
and his son Minoru, this was private property until 1946. Then it was taken over
by the Irish National Stud Company, which raises horses there but keeps the
gardens in excellent condition for the pleasure of the public. The entire garden
is planned to symbolize the life of a man. As the guide takes us about, we see
the cave that represents how he emerged into life, then we follow his childish
wandering footsteps on meandering paths, face the choices he must make in his
youth between temptations and work, and so on till we see the chair—a clipped
shrub—in which he died, and the bamboo gate through which his soul fled. The

garden is beautifully planted with colorful flowers and shrubs here and there to give variety, and has excellent landscaped contours for charming vistas. It is open daily from 2 to 6 P.M.

Mt. Usher, Ashford, County Wicklow, Eire
(25 miles south of Dublin) (112, 113)

One of the loveliest gardens in Ireland, created as a hobby by three generations of merchants. There are so many rare plants here that one should buy the large booklet describing them all and really study them. Yet the 16-acre garden, through which a small stream runs, looks as if it had grown without the help of man. Every path opens up new delights, new fine views. It is open Monday to Friday from 9 to 6, except holidays.

Powerscourt, Enniskerry, County Wicklow, Eire
(12 miles southwest of Dublin) (23, 61, 71, 78, 79)

One of the most beautiful Italianate gardens in Europe, created in 1843. There are six terraces—the first 800 feet long—each paved in gray-and-black-pebble mosaic and bounded by brown wrought-iron railings with gilt trim. At each level there are statues and urns brought from Italy. At the bottom of the slope lies the Triton Pool, and beyond are the Wicklow Hills. There is also a Japanese Garden, a deer park, and a very high waterfall on the estate. The grounds are open daily from Easter to October from 10 to 5:30. Some bus tours go there.

England

Avebury Manor, Marlborough, Wiltshire, England
(80 miles due west of London) (96, 97)

The 16th-century manor house has been continuously occupied for 400 years and is also open to the public. The elaborate topiary gardens set off masses of tulips and later perennials. House and gardens are open daily from 2 to 6. Nearby are the extraordinary prehistoric monument stones dating from about 1800 B.C.

Blenheim Palace, Woodstock, Oxfordshire, England
(eight miles north of Oxford) (128)

At the back of this palace where Sir Winston Churchill was born lies a garden often called the "English Versailles." It consists of scrolled parterres with tiny boxwood hedges filled in by crushed brick, surrounding a beautiful series of shallow round pools draining into each other through small, almost invisible waterfalls. At one side of the building there is another old formal garden, which seems rather confused today and not at all like the earlier very beautiful designs pictured in the guidebook. Open from 1 to 6 on Monday, Tuesday, Wednesday and Thursday until July 27, then daily. Many bus tours.

Christ Church Memorial Garden, Oxford, England (26)

This is one of the many fine gardens surrounding the various colleges at Oxford. Others that should not be missed are those at Balliol and Corpus Christi. Open in the early afternoons during college sessions, and from 10 to 6 in vacations. Also see the University Botanic Garden founded in 1621, open from 12 to 2 but closed Sundays.

Derry and Tom's Department Store, London, England
(on Kensington High Street) (34)

A strange place to find three lovely gardens, on top of a city department store in an area covering 1¾ acres! There is a Spanish Garden, with columned loggia and much tiling surrounding the profusion of flowers; a Wild Garden, where one really feels lost in the woods at a small pool; and a Tudor Garden, with old-fashioned roses and other flowers in prim beds. They are open during store hours. Have tea or lunch on the terrace.

Eastlands, Weybridge, Surrey, England
(very near London) (15C, 76, 100)

The home of the widow of Warwick Deeping, famous novelist. The intimate flower garden was beautifully planned by him, with square topiary shrubs marking the corners, and fine ancient Italian urns here and there as centers of interest. There is also a grassy glen where Sarah Siddons and Fanny Kemble once gave outdoor plays. On Brooklands Lane. G.S.

19

Garsington Manor, Garsington Near Oxford, Oxfordshire, England
(14C, 66)

The house, now owned by Sir John and Lady Wheeler-Bennett, was built in 1580, using some old stone from the 14th-century monastery on the same site. The square flowerbeds hemmed in by box hedges and Irish yews are now filled with flowers. They may date back to the 14th century, when they were probably used for herbs and vegetables by the monks. There is also a large brick monastery dovecote, still in excellent condition. G.S.

Great Dixter, Northiam, Sussex, England
(eight miles northwest of Rye) (13C, 92, 127)

A splendid series of gardens designed by Lutyens, displaying early bulbs, fruit trees, fine herbaceous borders, dahlias, and large yew topiaries in the form of peacocks and geometric designs. Open daily from 2 to 5 except Mondays, but open Bank Holiday Mondays.

Great Fosters Hotel, Egham, Surrey, England
(about 15 miles west of London) (33, 75, 98)

The building was once the hunting lodge of Queen Elizabeth I, and contains much fine antique furniture and tapestries. The gardens consist of a formal topiary pattern, with clipped hedges surrounding flowers, punctuated with amusing topiary forms; a charming rose garden with a pool at its center; and flower borders beyond.

The Hall, Bradford-on-Avon, Wiltshire, England
(southeast of Bath) (31)

A very large private garden belonging to A. E. Moulton, Esq. Terraces, fine flower borders, and topiary hedges are to be seen, below an Elizabethan house. G.S.

Hampton Court Palace, London, Middlesex, England (3)

The palace, begun by Cardinal Wolsey in 1514 and then taken over by Henry VIII, is surrounded by a variety of beautiful gardens. To the left of the entrance is a fine rose garden. The enclosed Tudor Garden, Baroque Garden, and Water Garden can be admired from above through openings in clipped trees. The Broad Walk is lined with deep perennial borders almost half a mile long. There is a vivid Knot Garden of annuals between miniature hedges, a naturalized area for spring bulbs and summer lilies, and the Great Grape Vine, planted in 1769 and still bearing some 650 clusters a year. One can easily get lost in the Maze. Bus tours from London visit the palace regularly, but they allow little time for exploring the gardens. Weekdays from 9:30 to 6, Sunday 11 to 6.

Hascombe Court, Godalming, Surrey, England (32, 59)

A fine private garden belonging to Mr. and Mrs. C. C. Jacobs. The spring bulbs, glorious herbaceous borders extending both front and back from the house, the lovely pool garden, and the terrace are all well worth seeing. G.S.

Haseley Court, Little Haseley, Oxfordshire, England
(seven miles southeast of Oxford) (94)

The mansion now belongs to an American, Mrs. Nancy Lancaster, who comes from Virginia and flies the Confederate flag from her roof! The gardens are reminiscent of her home state also, with paths covered by high hedges, unexpected views of lovely flowers, and a truly American white lattice garden pavilion. The topiary garden at one end of the house, however, is a splendid example of this old English art, representing an entire chess board of clipped yew and box figures, decorated along the edges with choice succulents. G.S.

Hever Castle, Edenbridge, Kent, England
(midway between London and the south coast) (95)

This charming 13th-century moated castle was once the home of Anne Boleyn. It fell into decay in later years until restored by an American, William Waldorf Astor, at one time Ambassador to Italy. He placed many Italian sculptures and urns in the gardens. His grandson, The Hon. Gavin Astor, is the present owner. Besides the formal Italian garden, there are topiary chessmen cut in the old forms, a small rose garden, a maze, a rock garden, and fine pool areas. The gardens are open Wednesday, Sunday, and Bank Holiday Mondays from 1 to 7, also Saturdays in August and September.

Hidcote Manor Gardens, Chipping Campden, Gloucestershire, England
(northwest of Oxford) (58, 93)

One of the most beautiful and most famous of the small gardens in England. Created by an American, the late Major Lawrence Johnston, it is designed like a series of rooms in a house, each surrounded by hedges, each specializing in different flowers or color schemes. The Stilt Garden, of clipped hornbeams, is particularly striking. There are many unusual flowers here, and species of hypericum and lavender developed and named in these gardens. The gardens are open daily from 11 to 8, except Tuesday and Friday.

Kew Gardens, Kew, London, England
(one mile from Richmond) (25C, 73)

This world-famous garden is a park of 300 acres with collections of 45,000 different plant species and varieties. The rhododendron walk is particularly lovely, and there are fine greenhouses and a herbarium. The park is open daily from 10 to 8, the greenhouses from 1 to 4:50 weekdays, 1 to 5:50 Sunday.

Marsh Lock, Near Henley-on-Thames, Oxfordshire, England (17C)

This is one of the lovely gardens planted by the lock-keepers on the Thames to enhance the waterway and their houses. Each year prizes are awarded for the best-kept lock gardens.

New Place, Stratford-upon-Avon, Warwickshire, England (2)

There is a herb garden here planted in the remaining foundation walls of Shakespeare's last home. Next to this is a superb example of the Elizabethan Knot Garden, so called because the beds are hemmed in by tiny box hedges in patterns like ribbons and bowknots, every space filled solidly each year with well-chosen colorful annuals. Open weekdays from 9 to 6, Sunday 2 to 6.

Nymans Gardens, Handcross, Sussex, England (28C)

A world-famous series of special gardens: splendid herbaceous borders with unusual topiaries, a heather garden, a Japanese Garden, a garden of old-fashioned roses; a rock garden. Everywhere there are unusual plants, fine specimens, and ancient trees. Open Tuesday through Thursday, Saturday, Sunday, and Bank Holiday Mondays from 2 to 7. Tour buses from London.

Packwood House, Hockley Heath, Warwickshire, England
(near Henley-in-Arden, northwest of Stratford-upon-Avon) (30, 67, 74, 91)

The fine Tudor house here is also open to the public. There are very beautiful flower borders within an old brick wall, charming garden houses of brick marking the corners, also a sunken rose garden. The most extraordinary part of the grounds, however, is the group of great yews 25 feet high, which were planted over 300 years ago to represent the Sermon on the Mount: Christ, the disciples, and the multitude. Open Tuesday, Wednesday, Thursday, Saturday, and Bank Holiday Mondays from 2 to 7; Sundays 3 to 7.

The Priory, Hurley, Berkshire, England (99)

There is a lovely garden behind this old priory, maintained by the owners, who are most hospitable to strangers who might wish to see it.

Pusey House, Faringdon, Berkshire, England
(not far from Oxford) (12C)

The house was built in 1748 and is now owned by Michael Hornby, Esq. Magnificent herbaceous borders stretch along walls from each side of the house; there is a walled garden, a lake and wild garden, and an ornamental swimming pool area. G.S.

Queen Mary's Rose Garden, Regent's Park, London, England (41)

Approached through a splendid wrought-iron gateway, this lovely rose garden is a quiet haven for flower lovers. It is a circular sunken garden, with shrub roses in the center beds and garlands of climbers looped from post to post encircling the whole. Beyond lies an interesting rock garden, a begonia collection, and flower borders. Open daily.

Reddish House, Broad Chalke, Salisbury, Wiltshire, England
(south of Salisbury) (26C)

The home of the famous artist-photographer Cecil Beaton shows his great
talents in the grounds as well as in the small conservatory, where every plant
is effectively placed for color and design. From the higher benches one can get
the best views of gardens and rolling hills beyond. There are herbaceous borders
in front of the thatched cottage beside the house, a rose garden, a herb garden,
a small temple, and next to the house an amusing group of topiary shrubs. G.S.

Savill Garden, Windsor Great Park, Berkshire, England (7C)

This is a 25-acre section of Windsor Great Park, which comprises about
4,500 acres. Begun in the 18th century under George II, it is now one of the
loveliest gardens in England. Its perennial borders, 15 feet deep and miraculously
kept in constant bloom, are to my mind among the finest anywhere. There are
also water gardens, a rose garden, an Alpine Garden, and outstanding varieties
of trees and shrubs—especially rhododendrons and azaleas—throughout the
naturalized areas. There are whole collections of spring bulbs, hemerocallis,
lilies, Meconopsis, and primulas. Daily 10 to 6. Crown property.

Sissinghurst Castle, Sissinghurst, Cranbrook, Kent, England
(15 miles from Tunbridge Wells) (8C)

The extraordinarily lovely gardens here were created by the late Victoria
Sackville-West, author and famous garden expert, and her husband Sir Harold
Nicolson. The rose garden is interplanted with perennials to give later color.
There are gardens all of white, or yellow, or red. There is a herb garden, and
a little cottage garden. Wherever you look you will find unusual plants and
interesting combinations of color and form. Some call it the greatest garden in
England. Open daily from 10 to 7.

Syon House Gardening Centre, Brentford, Middlesex, England
(only nine miles from the center of London, easily reached by bus,
train, or underground) (72, 129)

A unique display of the best that the nurserymen and garden equipment suppliers of Great Britain have to offer. The setting is a stately park created 200 years ago by "Capability Brown" for the Dukes of Northumberland, so there are magnificent old trees. There are many model gardens, plantings at a lakeside, a large rose garden in front of the Duke's mansion, formal and informal flower and shrub borders—all covering 55 acres of the estate. The conservatory, built in 1820, is unique and contains a colorful display of house plants. Everything is labeled and purchases may be made at special places, but the overall effect is not that of a merchandising exhibit but of a handsomely laid out flowering park. Open from May 1 to October 31 from 10:30 to between 5 and 6:30, depending on the season.

Wisley Gardens, Ripley, Surrey, England
(on Route A-3 from London, easily reached by bus) (21C)

This showplace and experimental station of the Royal Horticultural Society has a tremendous variety of collections for study: alpines, heathers, primroses, rhododendrons, annuals, perennial borders, and a fine rose garden. A number of greenhouses also add to the attractions. Open every weekday to nonmembers of the Society from 10 to 7:30, Sundays only to members, from 2 to 5:30. Admission charge for nonmembers.

France

Bagatelle, Paris, France
(on the edge of the Bois de Boulogne, easily reached by bus) (51, 83)

These exquisite gardens—and the palace as well—were a gift of the Comte d'Artois to his sister-in-law, Marie Antoinette. To win a bet, he had both constructed in two months. There are thousands of bulbs in the spring, fine rhododendrons around the palace, a long perennial garden with pergola, a very decorative iris garden, and, the high point of all, a rose garden that must look today much as it did when created. The curved beds are filled with the finest modern roses, edged here and there with tree roses and ramblers on posts or festooned on wires. Tall conical yews and white statuary, well placed, make a beautiful picture. There are asters and chrysanthemums in the fall, with a great park surrounding the more formal plantings. Open daily.

25

Château de Chenonceaux, Loire Valley, France
(southeast of Tours) (4)

A typical formal French garden of curled parterre designs in boxwood, and conical topiaries, spreading in front of the 16th-century château along a stream. It is open daily from 9 to 12, 2 to 7.

Château de Vaux-Le-Vicomte, Maincy, France
(not more than an hour's drive southeast of Paris) (14, 118)

To my mind this is the most beautiful and fascinating of the historic gardens of France. It was the first one that Le Nôtre designed, done for Nicolas Fouquet, Louis XIV's Finance Minister. When he saw it the King became so jealous that he imprisoned Fouquet for life and appropriated the château and gardens. There are great parterres in the center, varied with many pools and fountains, and "Secret Gardens" hedged in at the sides. The design leads the eye inevitably to the final great pool and the hill beyond with its statue on top. The gardens are open on Saturday and Sunday from 2 to 6, and on holidays.

Château de Versailles, France (13, 84, 85)

No visitor to France fails to take the bus tour from Paris to this world-famous palace and garden. If you want time to roam the grounds, however, it is better to go on your own, by train, bus, or car. The gardens were laid out by Le Nôtre as vast formal stage settings for royal parties, when thousands of pastel-colored gowns and satin suits would brighten the scene. There are smaller, circular pools, much statuary, and the great long basin, which extends almost farther than the eye can reach. The great fountains play only on certain Sundays in summer. Open daily except Tuesday, from 10 to 5.

Château de Villandry, Loire Valley, France
(southwest of Tours) (5, 6)

The finest garden of any of the Loire Valley châteaux. First planted in the 16th century, it is well restored in the original symbolic designs of clipped boxwood hedges. The pattern in each square in the foreground stands for a different kind of love: daggers and knives represent dangerous love; fans and butterflies,

26

frivolous love; hearts, wings, and arrows, passionate love; and a maze, foolish
love. Looking down on this fascinating garden from above, one can see beyond
it to the kitchen garden, where little rose arbors decorate the crossings of the
paths, and the vegetables are planted to make colorful patterns. The paths in
the hedge garden are raked into swirls and the public is not allowed on them.
Open daily from 9 to 12, 2 to 5:30 or 7.

Fleuriste Municipal, Paris, France
(3, Avenue Porte d'Auteuil) (54)

These 94 municipal greenhouses offer much to the garden enthusiast.
Some have collections of orchids or other flowers for later planting in the city
parks. Others are devoted to changing seasonal displays like the Azalea Show,
the Chrysanthemum Show, and the like. Open daily from 10 to 6.

Japanese Garden of Peace, Unesco Building, Paris, France (39)

This original yet authentically Japanese garden is located between the
Conference Building and the Delegates' Patio. It was designed by Isamu Noguchi,
an American citizen with a Japanese father, and was completed in 1958. Noguchi
is a sculptor, so his use of rocks, both in natural form and hewn shapes, is
particularly interesting. Like all Japanese gardens it represents a landscape in
miniature, with small hills, promontories, and raked sand areas representing
water. The magnolias, cherries, plums, and bamboos all came from Japan as
a gift of the government and are deliberately kept small. Open at all times.

Musée Île-de-France, St. Jean-Cap-Ferrat, France
(near the shoreline drive of the Côte d'Azur southeast of Nice) (33C)

Twelve acres of beautiful tropical gardens lie behind the museum building:
a Spanish Garden; an Exotic Garden; an Italian Garden; and others, all border-
ing the blue Mediterranean. Open daily from 3 to 7 except Monday.

Parc Floral D'Exposition Permanente, Orléans, France
(follow the signs "Parc Floral" in the city) (20C)

This is a unique permanent floral exposition, opened in 1964, a huge

27

series of model gardens displaying the products of the best nurserymen in France—something like the bulb display at Keukenhof in Holland. Famous especially for its rose gardens, the park also includes whole collections of iris, rhododendrons, dahlias, annuals, and perennials of many kinds. As every part is labeled, French visitors can note down where flowers they like can be obtained. Open daily from 8:30 to 7:30.

Germany

Berggarten, Hannover, Germany (22C)

A botanical garden adjacent to the historical Herrenhausen, well land-scaped with winding paths. There is a heather garden, demonstration flower borders for shade and sun, also many different plant collections. In the green-house, which was established in 1666, many foreign plants were first introduced to Europeans. Open daily from 8 to dusk.

Ettlingen, Germany (south of Karlsruhe) (30C)

The small canals in this quaint Black Forest town are decorated with gay flower boxes along all their fences, making a garden of the streets.

Gruga Park, Essen, Germany (23C)

One of the largest and finest parks in Germany, improved several times during a German Garden Show. Thousands of early bulbs, a valley of rhododen-drons, a water garden, and a series of sample home gardens are among its features. Loveliest of all is the "Dahlia Arena," completely filled with the finest varieties. A miniature railway facilitates seeing all sections of this fine park. Open daily.

Herrenhausen, Hannover, Germany (29C, 9, 10, 11, 43, 80, 130)

The most beautiful baroque garden in Germany, kept exactly as it was when it was created for the Hannoverian kings in 1680. The entrance is between rows of 1,300 great lime trees planted in 1727. There is a vast expanse of elaborate parterres, some filled with flowers, others with gravel in various colors. Beyond that lie a whole series of "Secret Gardens" within high hedges, each with its own specialized planting: roses, small topiary animals in softly tinted flowerbeds, a pool garden, a knot garden, and so on. At one side is the outdoor Garden Theatre, where concerts and ballets are performed on summer evenings. The Bell Fountain with its 167 sprays, and the "Great Fountain," the tallest in Germany, are illuminated at night. Open daily from 8 until dusk.

Island of Mainau, Lake Constance, Germany (45, 46)
(easily reached in 25 minutes by regular boat
service from Meersburg, or on foot by causeway from Constance)

One of the most beautiful gardens in Europe, owned by Count Lennart Bernadotte of Sweden, a renowned horticulturist. Many trees are now 200 years old. There is a tropical garden with bananas and oranges growing outdoors in the unusually mild climate. Some 600,000 bulbs bloom here in spring; then comes the beautifully designed rose garden; and these are followed by an extraordinary dahlia show in color-schemed irregular beds. Open daily from 7 to dusk.

Kurpark, Baden-Baden, Germany (44, 119)

This is an extensive park in the famous health resort on the edge of the Black Forest. The little bridges leading across a canal to some of the hotels and restaurants are gaily decorated with flower boxes. The rose garden, formal in design, is famous for its international competition judging.

Schlosspark, Ludwigsburg, Germany (north of Stuttgart) (3C)

The gardens in front of the 17th-century palace are planted in vivid parterre patterns, giving rise to the description of the park as "Flowering Baroque." Even lovelier is the large perennial garden in back, with fine flower borders reminiscent of some of the best in England. In spring these beds are planted with 50,000 tulips and hyacinths. There is also a rock garden, and an old parterre design of colored gravel visible only from the palace rooms. Open from 7 A.M. to 11 P.M.

Nordpark, Duesseldorf, Germany (20C, 121)

The citizens of this modern industrial city are justly proud of the Nordpark, with its extensive lawns, beautiful flower gardens, pools, and fountains. The terraces for resting and reading have interesting modernistic plant containers for decoration. There are a great variety of flowering shrubs and splendid borders of mixed conifers.

Pagodenburg, Rastatt, Germany (right on Highway #3 leading through the
northern part of the Black Forest to Freiburg) (28)

A charming little garden with narcissus and other early bulbs in spring, then a profusion of roses, followed by other flowers through the summer and fall. Going past the tiny old chapel one comes to a miniature palace, copied from one at Nymphenburg in Munich, which was built in 1772 by the archduchess as a playhouse for her grandchildren! Open daily in flowering season.

Palmengarten, Frankfurt/Main, Germany (19C, 24C, 27C, 55)

Perhaps the most famous and beloved park in Germany, really a botanical garden with much for the serious horticulturist. Ornamental borders, a rock garden, a very lovely rose garden with fountains, and parklike areas with a lake comprise the outdoor attractions. The greenhouses are outstanding, one, a huge glass building filled with tropical trees and ferns, having given the garden its name. Others contain outstanding collections of gloxinias, fuchsias, cacti, orchids, and begonias, hundreds of each kind. In one house exhibits are changed each month. Open daily.

Schloss Augustusburg, Bruehl, Germany (about eight miles south of Cologne)
(20)

A French-style formal palace garden designed by a pupil of Le Nôtre. There are large pools with fountains, surrounded by low boxwood parterres planted with pansies in the spring. There is also a little side garden filled with heliotrope in the summer. The 18th-century baroque palace of the archbishops is splendidly furnished and well worth a tour. Open daily.

30

Westfalenpark, Dortmund, Germany (120)

Right in the industrial Ruhr section, with its smoke and grime, the city fathers have provided their citizens with a glorious park area, extended several times when the triennial German Garden Show was located there. Brilliant with spring bulbs, followed by expanses of annuals and perennials, the park also features a delightful hillside Japanese Garden with authentic tea house, a rosarium, and illuminated fountains playing in harmony with symphonic organ concerts. Open daily.

Holland

Japanese Garden In Clingendael Park, The Hague, Holland (18C, 40)

From the bamboo roofed gateway past the moss garden and through the many winding paths, this garden is a constant delight. It is carefully planted for color accents with Japanese maples, primulas, and azaleas, which reflect in the tiny stream and pool. The authentic tea house with its purification basin, and the red lacquer bridge and occasional stone lanterns create a truly Japanese atmosphere. It is open only in May and to June 15th, 8 A.M. to 8 P.M., free, but one must get a permit through one's hotel porter or by mail from the park department: Gemeenteplantsoenen, Huygenspark 32, Postbus 1240, Den Haag.

Kasteel De Geldersche Toren, Spankeren, Gelderland, Holland (35)

This 16th-century private castle has beautiful flower borders in the garden. It is open to visitors only once a year when there is a two-day flower arrangers' competition either the last weekend in July or the first in August. Ask at Tourist Office (NVV).

Kasteel Twickel, Delden, Holland (near the northeastern border) (109)

One of the most beautiful gardens in Holland, all designed by the owner of the 14th-century moated castle, Baroness van Heeckeren van Wassenaar. The tiny Baroness, now 90, still supervises every planting and makes many changes each year to improve the color combinations and arrangement of heights in her flowerbeds. There are a superb English garden of mixed borders, a French topiary garden, a rock garden, and a rose garden. The rhododendrons everywhere on the estate are a great sight in May. Open Wednesday and Friday afternoons.

Keukenhof, Lisse, Holland (5C)

A beautifully designed park of 65 acres show-casing each May some seven million of the newest varieties of Holland's bulb growers. Great beds of tulips of every variety, narcissus, hyacinths, and smaller flowers are tastefully displayed in irregular beds along brook or pool, accented by charming fountains. Only half an hour from Amsterdam, special buses come from all over Holland during the blooming season. Open all day from late March into mid-May.

Peace Palace, The Hague, Holland (64)

At one side of this famous palace there is an unusually lovely garden, planted mostly with roses beside a long pool, but varied here and there with perennial borders. Open Monday through Saturday from 10 to 12, 1:30 to 4:40; Sunday 2 to 6.

Westbroekpark, The Hague, Holland (easily reached by trolley from the center of town) (81)

A lovely extensive park where one walks on broad lawns to admire the perennial borders, the rose garden (and a special place where international judging of roses takes place annually), the rock garden and pool, a garden of tiny roses, and much more. There is always color there. Open daily.

Zaanse Schans, Zaandam, Holland (22, 82)

This is a small village of quaint 18th-century wooden houses brought here from the surrounding area. Each house has been modernized inside and is lived in. Visitors see only the exteriors, the little gardens planted in the style of the period, and the interiors of the restaurant building (another period piece) and the old windmill where spices are ground and sold. The village is on some of the bus tours.

Zuiderpark, The Hague, Holland (42)

A fine decorative rose garden, and unusual trees of over 1,000 varieties make this park well worth a visit. Open daily.

Italy

La Mortola, Villa Hanbury, Ventimiglia, Italy (near the French border on the Mediterranean, can be reached by bus from San Remo) (89)

This is a garden of many rare plants imported from all over the world by Sir Thomas Hanbury, beginning in 1867. It lies on a steep hillside, with paths meandering back and forth through the fine landscaping. Open daily.

Palazzo Rufolo, Ravello, Italy (1C)

The palace itself dates from the 13th century, and the courtyard patio garden is of that period. But there seem to be no records of when the gay flower garden was designed. Looked at from the terrace above, it resembles a large mosaic of bright annuals planted in a prim pattern that is almost Victorian in feeling. Beyond lies the blue Mediterranean. Richard Wagner is said to have been inspired by these gardens to compose his "Home of the Flower Maidens" in the opera "Parsifal." A high spot on a flower-lover's tour of the Amalfi Drive. Open daily.

San Paolo (St. Paul's Without The Walls), Rome, Italy (48)

Adjacent to this famous church that is filled with art treasures, there is a small monastery and rose garden, the soft yellow of the walls and columned walkways surrounding it with grace and old-world atmosphere. Open daily, often on guided tours.

Vatican Gardens, Rome, Italy (25)

The very old parts of these gardens have practically disappeared, but the 20th-century grounds are very neatly kept. There is an interesting rock garden, parterres, and so on. Permission to see them must be asked for in writing at least four days in advance, from the Segretaria della Commissione Ponteficia per la Città Vaticano, or telephone them at 555–251.

Villa Carlotta, Cadenabbia, Lake Como, Italy (10C, 21, 32C)

This hillside garden facing beautiful Lake Como is a botanist's delight, for it is planted with trees and shrubs from all over the world. Its greatest attraction is the great azalea walk, which blooms in April and May. A booklet of the plantings is available. The interior of the villa may also be visited. Property of the Italian government, open daily. Bus tours.

Villa D'Este, Tivoli, Italy (a short distance from Rome) (123, 124, 125, 126)

A vast garden of old trees and open spaces, famous for its great variety of beautiful fountains and waterfalls. Some are made into fine spectacles with water rising and falling to and from great heights in combination; others are slender sprays in single pools; still others are small, like the famous row of 100 fountains spouting from a moss-covered wall. The sound of falling water and the fresh fragrance of wet earth, mosses, and ferns pervade the air. It is a startling show when the main water features are lighted at night. Open daily from 9 to one hour before sunset, and Tuesday, Thursday, Saturday, and Sunday till 11:30 P.M. Bus tours.

Villa Gamberaia, Settignano, Italy (a suburb of Florence) (15, 132, 133)

A world-famous garden, first laid out in 1610, beautifully designed with a center path and six pools. The plantings of clipped shrubs and hedges and the placing of red geraniums for accents—all are perfection. At the far end a long row of yews clipped in Spanish fashion into arches forms the background, while the sides are framed with other interesting topiary forms. Beside the house there is an ancient shell grotto. Ask at the cottage at the entrance for permission to see the garden.

Villa Garzoni, Collodi, Italy (northeast of Lucca) (88, 131)

An unusual formal Italian garden because it is a riot of colorful baroque flowerbeds instead of a picture in shades of green. The patterned beds and pools lie in front of an elaborately ornamented 17th-century staircase, leading to terraces from which one can view colors below. The surrounding high yew hedges are clipped like castle battlements. Open daily from 8 to 8.

Villa I Tatti, Settignano, Italy (69, 86, 87)

This former home of the famous art expert, Bernard Berenson, was willed to Harvard University upon his death as an institute for the study of Mediterranean art. The garden, though modern, has been designed in the tradition of the old Italian formal gardens. The walks are of interesting pebble mosaic design and there are geometric box hedges and lemon trees in terra-cotta pots. It all seems centuries old. Included in Garden Tours of the Tourist Bureau in Florence, as Settignano is a suburb of this city.

Villa Lante Di Bagnaia, Viterbo, Italy (about 75 miles southeast of Siena) (7, 122)

One of the finest examples of a 16th-century Italian garden to be seen today. It has been very well kept up. There are pools surrounded by balustrades with statue fountains and elaborate parterre patterns of miniature boxwood filled in with crushed brick. A high terrace above the garden makes it possible to look down and enjoy the design as a whole. There is also a rose garden, and a number of the "surprise fountains" that were so popular at that time, when the host would suddenly drench his guests from unsuspected sources. Open from 9:30 to 12:30, 3:30 to 7.

Villa La Pietra, Florence, Italy (110)

A beautiful example of a 17th-century Italian garden created by the late Arthur Acton, an Englishman. The formal designs and constant surprising vistas from one small hedged unit to the next are delightful. Most charming of all is the typical "green theatre," with its clipped shrubs representing the footlights and prompter's box in front, the wings in back setting off enchanting white statues of actors in period costume. On the Garden Tours of the local Tourist Bureau.

Villa Pallavicino, Stresa, Lago Maggiore, Italy (56, 65)

The extensive flower gardens and small zoo are the hobbies of the Marquesa de Pallavicino, who generously opens them to the public. There are beautiful beds of annuals and perennials, a little pool garden, and a greenhouse. In the zoo one may enter many of the enclosures to pet the deer, llamas, and other animals. Open daily.

Monaco

Exotic Garden, Monte Carlo, Monaco (49)

This "Jardin Exotique" is a fantastic place to visit. The paths wind back and forth down a steep hill, with giant cacti sending their branches high overhead and with grotesque forms of other cacti and succulents everywhere—some in bloom, some crawling like snakes on the ground—displaying a great variety of colors. At the base are grottoes of stalactites—a shivery contrast to the tropical heat of the garden. Open daily.

Northern Ireland

Creevy Rocks, Saintfield, County Down, Northern Ireland (11 miles northeast of Belfast) (6C)

Major D. Anderson has planted his entire garden area around the outcroppings of rocks, taking advantage of much wild yellow gorse for color, and contrasting it with flowers in blues and other shades in low irregular beds. Ask the National Trust in Belfast to arrange permission to see it if it is not already on a Garden Scheme tour list.

Guincho, Helen's Bay, County Down, Northern Ireland (east of Belfast) (16C)

Mrs. Frazer Mackie, owner and creator of this wonderful garden, is an expert plantsman. Everything there is unusual, and in excellent condition. From the heather borders in front of the house to the flower and shrub borders leading to a woods garden, there is something to admire at every step. Ask the National Trust in Belfast to make an appointment.

Mt. Stewart, Newtownards, County Down, Northern Ireland (ten miles east of Belfast) (60, 77, 101, 102)

A whole series of extensive gardens designed by the Marchioness of Londonderry, including the humorous animals of stone that add so much to the charm of the grounds. There is a large Italianate garden with pool in front of the house, a sunken Spanish Garden, a blue-and-white Mairi Garden, a Peace Garden with graves of family pets, a Rhododendron Walk, and a garden in the shape of a shamrock, with a topiary Irish harp and parades of animals clipped from the tops of the tall hedges. Open Monday, Wednesday, Saturday, Sunday and Bank Holiday Mondays, from 2 to 6. A booklet describes the plants in each garden.

Rowallane, Saintfield, County Down, Northern Ireland (11 miles northeast of Belfast) (27)

The grounds were laid out and thousands of trees planted in 1864 by the Reverend John Moore. Everywhere are flowering shrubs, many varieties having been hybridized here, especially a Viburnum tomentosum, primulas, hypericum, and some specimens in the undulating borders of rhododendrons for which the gardens are especially famous. There is also a truly English walled flower garden and a fine rock garden. Buy the garden guide to identify the many lovely plantings in this extensive place. Open daily from 9 to 6.

Portugal

Quinta Da Bacalhoa, Villa Fresca De Azeitao, Portugal (25 miles south of Lisbon on the road to Setubal) (1)

This beautiful 15th-century palace and garden were in ruins when an American, Mrs. Herbert Scoville, bought it in 1936 and started a careful restoration. The boxwood hedges of the garden have been copied from old Moorish designs. Everywhere are tiled fountains and walls, and there is a long tiled pavilion and loggia along a great pool with frequent views of the water through the arches. Write to Mrs. Scoville in advance at the above address for permission to visit.

Quinta De Marquez De Fronteira, Bemfica, Portugal (Bemfica is a suburb of Lisbon) (2C, 16, 136)

This 17th-century Portuguese garden is the finest example of its kind to be seen today. Two great blue-and-white tiled staircases lead up to a terrace topped by red-roofed towers. From here one can view the very large basin below, and the intricate maze pattern of the low clipped hedges in the garden, the white statues, and the topiary shrubs. The tiling around the pool pictures historic knights; above are busts of all the kings of Portugal to the time the garden was created. In other parts of the garden there is a tiled bench with an amusing tale of a cat teaching music to a group of monkeys. Open daily, but ask the American Express office for hours.

Royal Palace, Queluz, Portugal (19)

The pink stucco 18th-century palace is still used for official receptions. Eisenhower and many other notables were entertained in the beautiful rooms, which are open to the public. The gardens are in formal geometric shapes, with hedges filled with pink begonias and petunias, statuary, and blue-and-white urns; there is a large pool at one side. Open daily except Monday, from 10 to 5. On bus tours.

Scotland

Cawdor Dastle, Cawdor, Nairn, Scotland (8)

This is the castle where Macbeth is said to have been murdered. It is now the home of the Earl of Cawdor and Lady Cawdor. A splendid example of ancient Scottish forts, it was begun in 1396, and the square tower and parts of the Curtain Wall of this period are still standing. The lime trees were planted in 1680 and the walled garden was laid out at the same time. The flower garden outside the wall has been kept just as it was designed in 1820–1830.

Crarae Lodge, Minard, Argyll, Scotland (115)

Sir Ilay Campbell, following in the footsteps of his father, Sir George I. Campbell, has supervised the creation of an exceptionally beautiful garden in a highland glen. Although looking as if nature had done all the planting, the choice rhododendrons and azaleas along the banks of a small stream were actually placed there with landscaping skill. The paths rove up and down hill, with small rustic bridges here and there so that one may get views from both sides. There is also an extremely fine arboretum of eucalyptus and conifers. Although May and June are the most colorful months, the garden is open daily from dawn to dusk between April and October. Bus from Glasgow goes to the door.

Earlshall, Leuchars, Fife, Scotland (103, 104)

A small, beautifully restored 16th-century castle is surrounded by lovely flower gardens and fascinating groupings of ancient topiary shapes. Easily reached by bus from St. Andrews. S.G.S.

Kinross House, Kinross, Kinross-Shire, Scotland (105)

A large rose garden leads down to the lake view of Loch Leven Castle. The surrounding wall has interesting yew hedge dividers between plantings of perennials. A very lovely 17th-century garden. Easily reached by bus. S.G.S.

Park On Princes Street, Edinburgh, Scotland (50)

Every visitor to this famous city visits the Sir Walter Scott monument at one end of the park along the popular shopping street. Nearby is the Floral Clock made each year of variegated succulent forms, and beyond are wall flowers and other plantings.

Pittencrieff Glen, Dunfermline, Kinross-Shire, Scotland (53)

This park of 60 acres was given by Dunfermline's native son, Andrew Carnegie. There are well-designed flower beds and rock gardens and a small greenhouse. Open daily.

Alhambra, Granada, Spain (134, 135)

The garden spots of this 14th-century Moorish pleasure palace are as beautiful as the red stone buildings. There are pools and flowers, tall clipped hedges, and pointed cypresses, along with intricately patterned mosaic walks leading from one lovely spot to another. In the park are elms planted by the Duke of Wellington in the early 19th century. Open daily.

Generalife, Granada, Spain (70, 111)

In contrast to the red buildings of the Alhambra, this Moorish palace complex is a creamy white, and contains many more gardens. Some authorities say that the name (pronounced hen-eh-ra-lee-fay) means "Sublime Garden," and it well deserves this title. It is supreme among Spanish gardens. Open daily.

Marimurtra, Blanes, Spain (on the coast not far from the French border) (68, 90)

A botanical garden maintained by the Carlos Faust Foundation. Designed for beauty as well as study, the numbered signs insure that a visitor will not miss any of the many paths with their well-marked tropical flower and foliage displays, the exotic tiled lotus pool, or the many framed-in views of the blue Mediterranean beyond. Open daily from 9 to 7.

Switzerland

Municipal Succulent Collection (Staetdische Sukkulentensammlung), Zurich, Switzerland

This outstanding collection in seven greenhouses and 13 outdoor display cases, sponsored by the International Succulent Society, is a "must" for gardeners interested in this specialty. There are 4,500 different succulents from all over the world. Open all year. Mythenkai 88, along the lake front.

One of the loveliest rose gardens in Europe, the design is varied with pools, a pergola on a mound, statuary, and clipped shrubs. Some 12,000 shrub roses of 180 varieties are on display, the whole illuminated as a fairyland picture at night.

Wales

Bodnant Gardens, Tal-Y-Cafn, Denbighshire, Wales (four miles south of Conway) (4C)

These glorious gardens were laid out in 1875 by the grandfather of Lord Aberconway, who still supervises the property. From the yellow arches of the laburnum walk, to the various flowered terraces looking out over the valley to the Snowdonia range, and on down into the famous ravine covered with hybrid rhododendrons, the gardens are a continuous delight. Open April to October, Tuesday, Wednesday, Thursday, Saturday, and Bank Holiday Mondays, from 1:30 to 4:45. Many bus tours go there.

Chirk Castle, Wrexham, Denbighshire, Wales (two miles from Chirk on A5;
20 miles northwest of Shrewsbury, England;
seven miles south of Llangollen)
(12, 63, 107)

The castle itself was built in 1310, and can be visited. It has been inhabited continuously for 650 years, the last 300 by Col. Myddelton's family. There is a large croquet lawn at the side, lined with enormous topiaries, with a topiary hedge clipped in crenellations like the castle walls. Beyond lie lovely flower gardens, a rose garden, and a rock garden. Open Easter weekend and May through September on Tuesday, Thursday, Saturday, and Sunday from 2 to 5. Many bus tours go there.

Gwydyr Castle, Llanwrst, Denbighshire, Wales (not far from the famous village of Betws-y-Coed) (108)

A historical Royal Residence of Tudor days, with a rose garden (unfor-

tunately often attacked by the peacocks!) and splendid old yew topiaries. Open
daily from 9:30 to dusk.

Powis Castle, Welshpool, Montgomeryshire, Wales (on Route 483 to Newtown;
19 miles west of Shrewsbury, England) (17, 18, 106)

A splendid terraced late-17th-century Italianate garden drops off a steep
hillside, each level lined with flowerbeds on one side, balustrades and statues on
the other. There is a tremendous yew hedge down the incline over 30 feet high
and more than 200 years old. Some of the topiary yews have trunks two feet in
diameter. The view of the valley is superb. The interior of the medieval castle,
still inhabited by the Earl of Powis, can also be visited. Open from 1 to 6 except
Monday and Tuesday. A booklet lists all plantings.

Royal Floral Hall, Rhyl, Wales (on the north coast, (52)

This is a landscaped garden under a glass roof. Great masses of delicate
Schizanthus almost fill one wall. Everywhere are varieties of fuchsias, with a
special display case at the entrance giving the name of each variety; and a booklet
is available with directions for their care. Open daily from 10 to 8.

2

SOME HISTORIC GARDENS
AS THEY LOOK TODAY

(PRESENTED CHRONOLOGICALLY BY CENTURY)

1. QUINTA DA BACALHOA, VILLA FRESCA DE AZEITAO, PORTU-GAL. Boxwood hedges, recreated in the 15th-century designs originally planted at this royal palace, surround a typical Portuguese tiled fountain.

2. NEW PLACE, STRATFORD-UPON-AVON, WARWICKSHIRE, ENG-LAND. *Detail of the Knot Garden showing the small box hedges in loops around blossoming sedums and other plants.*

3. *HAMPTON COURT PALACE, LONDON, MIDDLESEX, ENGLAND.*
One of the authentic Tudor gardens of the time of Henry VIII. The formal parterre is filled in with red begonias.

4. CHÂTEAU DE CHENONCEAUX, LOIRE VALLEY, FRANCE. *This 16th-century château is surrounded by a formal garden of small boxwood hedges in scrolled parterres, accented with dome-shaped topiaries.*

5. *CHÂTEAU DE VILLANDRY, LOIRE VALLEY, FRANCE. The intricate designs of these 16th-century clipped boxwood hedges symbolize four kinds of love. The heart shapes in the foreground stand for passionate love. In spring these forms are filled in with tulips and forget-me-nots.*

6. *CHÂTEAU DE VILLANDRY, LOIRE VALLEY, FRANCE. This detail of the hedges in the shape of butterflies and fans symbolizes frivolous love.*

7. *VILLA LANTE DI BAGNAIA, VITERBO, ITALY. Perhaps the finest example of a 16th-century garden to be seen in Italy today. The blue sky reflects in the balustraded pools. The intricate parterre patterns are filled in with crushed brick to make a colorful design.*

8. *CAWDOR CASTLE, NAIRN, SCOTLAND. Lady Cawdor still keeps the design of this walled garden (seen from the 14th-century castle tower) as it was when laid out in 1680. In the foreground are four large oval beds with a delicate little arbor at their center; beyond one sees two formal rectangular gardens accented by tall pointed cypresses. The lime trees nearby were also planted in 1680.*

9. *HERRENHAUSEN, HANNOVER, GERMANY. Part of the vast expanse of the bedding designs near the entrance of this 17th-century garden. They are outlined with miniature box hedges, and filled in with low annuals— alyssum, ageratum, and other colorful flowers. White urns and statues mark the corners.*

10. HERRENHAUSEN, HANNOVER, GERMANY. *This checkerboard garden of low boxwood outlines appears exactly as it did in 17th-century pictures, the alternate squares marked with clay-potted lemon trees.*

11. HERRENHAUSEN, HANNOVER, GERMANY. *A detail of the geometric parterre design, so modern in feeling that it seems to belie its 17th-century origin. It is filled in with gravel instead of flowers, in white, pink, and dark gray, outlined in narrow boxwood.*

12. CHIRK CASTLE, WREXHAM, DENBIGHSHIRE, WALES. The huge topiaries on the side lawn of this 17th-century castle are ancient too.

13. *CHATEAU DE VERSAILLES, FRANCE. Green parterres surrounded by conical topiaries and several pools form a small part of this vast garden designed by Le Nôtre for King Louis XIV.*

14. *CHATEAU DE VAUX-LE-VICOMTE, MAINCY, FRANCE. The first garden designed by the great Le Nôtre, it seems to epitomize his extraordinary genius for formal design. The picture shows only part of a grandiose variety of gardens.*

15. VILLA GAMBERAIA, SETTIGNANO, ITALY. The lovely design of this garden, one of the finest examples of 17th-century landscaping in Italy today, as viewed from the upper porch of the villa, built for just this purpose. A great variety of topiaries accent the pools, which are brightened by red geraniums here and there.

16. *QUINTA DE MARQUEZ DE FRONTEIRA, BEMFICA, PORTUGAL. A
detail of the tiled pictures of fighting knights that surround the great pool
of this superb 17th-century garden.*

17. *POWIS CASTLE, WELSHPOOL, MONTGOMERYSHIRE, WALES.*
One of the five balustraded terraces of this 18th-century garden.

18. POWIS CASTLE, WELSHPOOL, MONTGOMERYSHIRE, WALES.
The dividing wall of one of the Italianate terraces is topped by ancient yew
topiaries. In the foreground is a fine lead statue of a peacock.

19. *ROYAL PALACE, QUELUZ, PORTUGAL. The pink of the 18th-century stucco building is repeated in the petunias and begonias within the box hedges, also in the rosy geraniums in tall ceramic urns.*

20. *SCHLOSS AUGUSTUSBURG, BRUEHL, GERMANY. The formal gardens were designed by a pupil of Le Nôtre. In the spring, edgings of pansies add color and soften the severe lines of the parterres and the conical shrubs.*

1C. PALAZZO RUFOLO, RAVELLO, ITALY. *Though the first courtyard garden at this lovely palace is still medieval in character, the brightly patterned flowerbeds along the Mediterranean shore look almost Victorian. Each bed is filled with a different annual: petunias, ageratum, marigolds, and the like.*

2C. QUINTA DE MARQUEZ DE FRONTEIRA, BEMFICA, PORTUGAL *An outstanding example of a 17th-century Portuguese garden. The blue and-white tiled staircases lead to the terrace from which one can view the intricate maze of boxwood, the white statues and the topiary shrubs. Between the stairs lies a long tiled pool.*

3C. SCHLOSSPARK, LUDWIGSBURG, GERMANY. The extensive flower parterres of this park in front of the 17th-century palace have been named "Bluehendes Barock" (Blossoming Baroque) by the Germans.

4C. BODNANT, TAL-Y-CAFN, WALES. The trees in this 19th-century garden are justly famous. A tall Embothrium *from Chile is covered with red blossoms, rhododendrons filling the spaces below.*

21. *VILLA CARLOTTA, CADENABBIA, LAKE COMO, ITALY. The
beautiful fountain at this 18th-century villa lies in front of the graceful staircases, which are ornamented with vines and small potted junipers.*

22. *ZAANSE SCHANS, ZAANDAM, HOLLAND. A recreated home garden of the 18th century in this small restored village.*

23. *POWERSCOURT, ENNISKERRY, COUNTY WICKLOW, EIRE. This glorious Italianate garden was created in the 19th century. The large Triton Pool with its twin horses taken from the family coat-of-arms lies at the foot of descending staircases. Sugar Loaf Mountain forms a magnificent backdrop.*

24. *GARINISH ISLAND, GLENGARRIFF, COUNTY CORK, EIRE. The formal cream-yellow loggia at the far end of the Italian Garden frames a view of the bay and the misty mountains beyond. At the foot of the steps, forget-me-nots and red tulips brighten the spring scene. Potted Japanese bonsai and other small trees are placed along the patterned brick wall surrounding the central pool.*

25. *VATICAN GARDENS, ROME, ITALY. This is the 20th-century part of the gardens made of grassy islands between automobile roads, decorated with palms and statuary. The picture was taken from the top of St. Peter's dome.*

3

FLOWER GARDENS

26. CHRIST CHURCH MEMORIAL GARDEN, OXFORD, OXFORD-SHIRE, ENGLAND. *A delicate rock garden of forget-me-nots, wall flowers, and candytuft* (Iberis), *with tulips above.*

27. *ROWALLANE, SAINTFIELD, COUNTY DOWN, NORTHERN IRE-LAND. A lovely bed of varicolored tulips in the Walled Garden. The brick wall has an interesting pattern. On the gate posts are old stone ball orna-ments, and from the little house in the corner one may view the entire garden.*

28. PAGODENBURG, RASTATT, GERMANY. *The lawn has been carefully clipped around the winding trail of narcissus on one side, tulips on the other, leading to the 18th-century chapel.*

5C. KEUKENHOF, LISSE, HOLLAND. A charming corner of this great park where Holland's bulb growers display their newest varieties each year.

6C. CREEVY ROCKS, SAINTFIELD, COUNTY DOWN, NORTHERN IRELAND. Major Anderson's garden is skillfully planted around natural outcroppings of rock. A small double gorse in the foreground repeats the color of the wild gorse in back, making a pleasing contrast to the masses of blue Lithospermum.

8C. *SISSINGHURST CASTLE, CRANBROOK, KENT, ENGLAND. A quaint corner with a lovely color scheme. The rose "Mme. Alfred Carrière" on the wall;* Venidio-arctotis, "Flame," *at left and right; and at the far right,* Alstroemeria. *In the right foreground are* Cheiranthus, Gazania, *and German iris.*

7C. *SAVILL GARDEN, WINDSOR GREAT PARK, BERKSHIRE, ENGLAND. Delphiniums eight feet tall in the border, with Red-hot Poker* (Kniphofia) *and sweet peas in the foreground.*

9C. *GLASNEVIN BOTANICAL GARDENS, DUBLIN, EIRE. One of the famous wide perennial borders, each plant carefully marked. The purple flower in the foreground is* Salvia campanula, *with lavender phlox behind it.*

_C. VILLA CARLOTTA, CADENABBIA, LAKE COMO, ITALY. An un-
usual tropical flower border accented by a banana tree and two varieties
of palms._

_11C. PARC FLORAL D'EXPOSITION PERMANENTE, ORLÉANS,
FRANCE. A striking border of lupines in this demonstration garden by
France's nurserymen._

_12C. PUSEY HOUSE, FARINGDON, BERKSHIRE, ENGLAND. One of
the borders in the Walled Garden, vivid with snapdragons (Antirrhinums),
Verbenas, geraniums, pentstemons, dahlias, and the roses "Frencham" and
"John Osborne."_

13C. GREAT DIXTER, NORTHIAM, SUSSEX, ENGLAND. *A striking deep red hydrangea beside an absolutely clear white one makes an unusual garden picture.*

14C. GARSINGTON MANOR, GARSINGTON NEAR OXFORD, OXFORDSHIRE, ENGLAND. *In each of the square beds—possibly laid out by monks in the 14th century for herbs and vegetables—there are different annuals and tree roses. Small box hedges and Irish yews surround the units.*

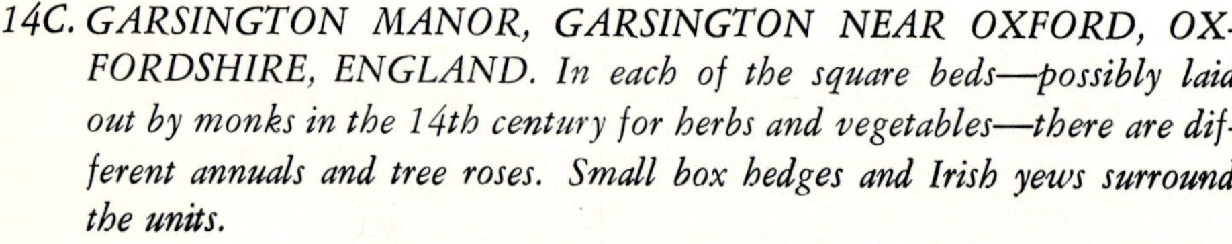

15C. EASTLANDS, WEYBRIDGE, SURREY, ENGLAND. *One of the beautiful terra-cotta urns collected in Italy by the Warwick Deepings, surrounded by dark red bergamot, begonias, and yellow daisies.*

29. GAVNØ MANOR, NEAR NAESTVED, ZEALAND, DENMARK. *A lovely mixed border in the English manner leads up to the typical half-timbered Danish cottage. Veronicas and tall delphiniums dominate the right-hand border, while the wall at the left is varied by espaliered fruit trees and inserts of colorful ceramics.*

30. *PACKWOOD HOUSE, HOCKLEY HEATH, WARWICKSHIRE, ENG-LAND. The warm red-brick wall and delightful corner garden houses from the 17th century frame in these beautiful perennial borders.*

31. THE HALL, BRADFORD-ON-AVON, WILTSHIRE, ENGLAND. *The wide flower borders above the lower walk are neatly hemmed in by low hedges, while a tall row of topiaries marches along the other side. Roses decorate the upper foreground terrace.*

32. *HASCOMBE COURT, GODALMING, SURREY, ENGLAND. The extraordinarily beautiful wide borders have been placed so that one may see them from the living-room windows. This is unusual in English home gardens, where the flowers as a rule are planted farther away from the house.*

33. *GREAT FOSTERS HOTEL, EGHAM, SURREY, ENGLAND. A color-ful dahlia garden is one of the charming hedged-in units here, with a bronze statue as the central focal point.*

34. DERRY & TOM'S DEPARTMENT STORE, LONDON, ENGLAND.
A colorful mixed border in the Spanish Garden high up on the roof contains yellow achillea, phlox, veronica, and dahlias in the background, helenium and other flowers in front. The planting is truly English, but one can see the tile edging of the beds and Spanish arches in the background.

35. *KASTEEL DE GELDERSCHE TOREN, SPANKEREN, GELDER-LAND, HOLLAND. There are colorful flower borders in the garden at one side of this ancient castle.*

16C. GUINCHO, HELEN'S BAY, COUNTY DOWN, NORTHERN IRE-
LAND. *The home of Mrs. Frazer Mackie looks out over an unusually
well-designed scroll-work of borders planted in various shades of heather.
Double gorse, developed from the wild variety, forms an edging near the
house.*

17C. MARSH LOCK, NEAR HENLEY-ON-THAMES, OXFORDSHIRE,
ENGLAND. *A colorful border of geraniums and small mounds of marigolds brighten this lock on the River Thames.*

4

SPECIALIZED GARDENS

A.   Japanese Gardens

18C. JAPANESE GARDEN IN CLINGENDAEL PARK, THE HAGUE, HOLLAND. This is beautifully designed, with a red lacquer bridge, a stone lantern, and a purification bowl in front of the tea house. Tall Primula Japonica *rim the pool.*

36. *JAPANESE GARDEN, KILDARE, COUNTY TULLY, EIRE. The red
lacquer bridge is flanked by a very fine Japanese stone lantern.*

37. *JAPANESE GARDEN, KILDARE, COUNTY TULLY, EIRE. A lovely stone lantern is surrounded by shrubs and trees deliberately selected for their variety of color and form.*

38. *JAPANESE GARDEN, KILDARE, COUNTY TULLY, EIRE. This entire garden symbolizes the Life of Man. At the end of the guided tour one sees this clipped boxwood representing the chair in which the old man died.*

39. *JAPANESE GARDEN OF PEACE, UNESCO BUILDING, PARIS, FRANCE. The fine design of this garden combines areas of grass and shrubs with others of pebbles and carved stones. These are separated by various pools and joined by stepping stones.*

40. *JAPANESE GARDEN IN CLINGENDAEL PARK, THE HAGUE, HOLLAND. A typical Japanese bridge of curved stone is carefully placed to reflect in the pond, surrounded by many ferns. The background is of Japanese maples and other small trees with delicate foliage.*

B.   Rose Gardens

41. QUEEN MARY'S ROSE GARDEN, REGENT'S PARK, LONDON, ENGLAND. *The sunken garden of shrub roses is surrounded by a higher grassy level. Here double garlands of climbers with others on supporting pillars make a colorful enclosure. The rose in the foreground is the pink "Mischief."*

42. ZUIDERPARK, THE HAGUE, HOLLAND. *A lovely view of the rose-beds and paths leading to a back wall of rose arbors.*

43. HERRENHAUSEN, HANNOVER, GERMANY. One of the "Secret Gardens" surrounded by a high hedge is filled with roses. At each corner is a quaint little summerhouse with dark gray arches and a white lattice domed roof, where one can sit and admire the profusion of bloom.

44. *KURPARK, BADEN-BADEN, GERMANY. This formal rose garden has stone urns filled with geraniums placed here and there as accents. In the distance the mountains of the Black Forest form a backdrop.*

45. ISLAND OF MAINAU, LAKE CONSTANCE, GERMANY. From May to June the 25,000 roses in this garden attract thousands of visitors.

46. *ISLAND OF MAINAU, LAKE CONSTANCE, GERMANY. Floribundas and tree roses, with a background of an old stone balustrade leading to a terrace.*

47. *PARC DE LA GRANGE, GENEVA, SWITZERLAND. A large pergola high on a terrace is a prominent feature of this rose garden, one of the prettiest in Europe.*

48. *SAN PAOLO (ST. PAUL WITHOUT THE WALLS), ROME, ITALY.*
The rose garden in the courtyard of the cloisters is surrounded by delicately wrought pillars and arches, and warm yellow walls.

20C. NORDPARK, DUESSELDORF, GERMANY. Part of the extensive rosebeds in one section of this fine park.

19C. PALMENGARTEN, FRANKFURT/MAIN, GERMANY. Floribundas and climbing varieties make this rose garden one of the loveliest features of this great botanical garden.

21C. WISLEY GARDENS, RIPLEY, SURREY, ENGLAND. One of the loveliest of hundreds of roses in this outstanding garden: the hybrid tea "Lucy Cramphorn."

22C. BERGGARTEN, HANNOVER, GERMANY. A beautiful Phyllocactus in the greenhouse is "Anton Guenther," which blooms from March to June, each blossom lasting several days.

49. EXOTIC GARDEN, MONTE CARLO, MONACO. Part of the steeply winding path wandering back and forth in a strange forest of huge cacti.

50. PARK ON PRINCES STREET, EDINBURGH, SCOTLAND. This famous floral clock is replanted each year in a delightful colored pattern of small succulents. Here one sees it just before completion and the placing of the minute and hour hands.

51. *MUNICIPAL SUCCULENT COLLECTION, ZURICH, SWITZER-LAND. A section of this very extensive collection. The creeping snake-like form is* Trichocereus thelegonus; *the ones in the center are* Sedum dasyphyllum; *the large round cacti in back,* Echinocactus Grussonii; *and the smaller round cactus in the foreground,* Ferocactus glaucescens.

D.   Dahlia Gardens

23C. GRUGA PARK, ESSEN, GERMANY. The most famous spot in this great park is the Dahlia Arena, a huge amphitheatre of colorful specimens of all the best varieties.

4C. PALMENGARTEN, FRANKFURT/ MAIN, GERMANY. A gorgeous specimen of Japanese iris in the iris garden.

E.   Iris Gardens

25C. *KEW GARDENS, KEW, LONDON, ENGLAND. One of the beautiful specimens on the Rhododendron Walk, Rhododendron occidentale.*

G.   Gardens Under Glass

26C. *REDDISH HOUSE, BROAD CHALKE, SALISBURY, WILTSHIRE, ENGLAND. A charming blue-and-white conservatory in the home of the famous artist-photographer, Cecil Beaton, designed by him. The small potted tree is a Eucalyptus.*

27C. *PALMENGARTEN, FRANKFURT/ MAIN, GERMANY. One of the conservatories featuring fuchsias above, gloxinias below.*

52. *ROYAL FLORAL HALL, RHYL, WALES. This landscaped greenhouse
has a whole wall of Schizanthus, its fluttering pink blossoms well deserving
its common name, butterfly-flower. Water trickles down the steps toward a
row of cockscomb (Celosia) and fuchsias hanging from the roof.*

53. PITTENCRIEFF GLEN, DUNFERMLINE, KINROSS-SHIRE, SCOT-LAND. The greenhouse in this park contains an amazing espaliered pink geranium some 12 feet high. Note the back of the chair in the foreground for comparison.

54. *FLEURISTE MUNICIPAL, PARIS, FRANCE. A fine collection of orchids in one of the municipal greenhouses.*

55. PALMENGARTEN, FRANKFURT/ MAIN, GERMANY. *This green-house pool is filled with the enormous leaves of the* Victoria regia, *a fragrant night-blooming South American water lily. It is said that the lilypads are so strong one could set a small child on one of them without his getting wet.*

56. *VILLA PALLAVICINO, STRESA, LAGO MAGGIORE, ITALY. The
Marquesa's greenhouse contains a fine primrose plant set on a beautiful
antique brass scale.*

5

GARDEN ORNAMENTS

57. *SISSINGHURST CASTLE, CRANBROOK, KENT, ENGLAND. The first glimpse one gets of these superb gardens is of tall clipped hedges seen through the castle gate. At the right is a honeysuckle vine (Lonicera Brownii fuchsiodes), which blooms from May to October.*

58. HIDCOTE MANOR GARDENS, CHIPPING CAMPDEN, GLOU-
CESTERSHIRE, ENGLAND. *A carefully placed wrought-iron gate gives
a magnificent view of an old Cedar of Lebanon. Lilacs on each side of the
gate fill the air with fragrance as one passes through.*

59. *HASCOMBE COURT, GODALMING, SURREY, ENGLAND. A stone gateway halfway along one of the great flower borders is ornamented with an appropriate della Robbia plaque of a gardener at work. This is surmounted with four curved rows of brick patterning.*

60. MT. STEWART, NEWTOWNARDS, COUNTY DOWN, NORTH-
ERN IRELAND. *One of the charms of this great series of gardens is the
constant change of levels and types of landscaping. This beautiful wrought-
iron gate marks one of the transitions.*

61. POWERSCOURT, ENNISKERRY, COUNTY WICKLOW, EIRE. *An extraordinary gate, as the design gives the effect of three-dimensional perspective. It originally came from Bamberg Cathedral in Germany.*

62. GLEN VEAGH, VEAGH, COUNTY DONEGAL, EIRE. *Looking through a gate from the wild garden to the mountains beyond.*

63. *CHIRK CASTLE, WREXHAM, WALES. The handsome entrance gate to the castle's beautiful grounds was made in 1719 and has been declared a National Monument.*

64. PEACE PALACE, THE HAGUE, HOLLAND. *Although this beautiful iron gate is not used as an entrance to the grounds, one can glimpse the colorful garden through it.*

65. *VILLA PALLAVICINO, STRESA, LAGO MAGGIORE, ITALY. A delicately wrought gate is flanked by stone posts and urns filled with geraniums. It leads to the small ornamental pool beyond.*

66. *GARSINGTON MANOR, GARSINGTON, OXFORDSHIRE, ENG-LAND. An 18th-century Italianate loggia that was added to the 16th-century house, with clever color accents of hydrangeas.*

67. *PACKWOOD HOUSE, HOCKLEY HEATH, WARWICKSHIRE, ENG-LAND. There are two theories about the use of the alcoves in these 17th-century brick walls. One is that they were small fireplaces to warm the walls and bring the espaliered fruit to earlier ripening. The other is that the big straw bee-hives were sheltered there in winter.*

68. MARIMURTA, BLANES, SPAIN. *An interesting combination of hedges and walls lines the stairway, each tier accented with small trees.*

69. *VILLA I TATTI, SETTIGNANO, ITALY. This formal topiary garden has a pathway decorated with pebble mosaic patterns in gray, rose, yellow, and white, descending by small terraces.*

70. GENERALIFE, GRANADA, SPAIN. *A decorative wide path of pebble mosaic in gray and white leads along the flower borders and trees.*

71. POWERSCOURT, ENNISKERRY, COUNTY WICKLOW, EIRE.
Among the most beautiful features of this superb Italianate garden are the terraces leading down to the large pool. Each is paved with rounded stones in gray and white, framed in by brown and gold ironwork railings.

72. *SYON HOUSE GARDENING CENTRE, BRENTFORD, MIDDLE-SEX, ENGLAND. The central sculpture of this model garden is a charming 19th-century French musician. The garden, created by the magazine* Woman's Realm, *demonstrates what can be done in landscaping small home grounds.*

*73. KEW GARDENS, KEW, LONDON, SURREY, ENGLAND. A delight-
fully appropriate bronze statue of a gardener in his working clothes, repre-
sentative of the more than 200 men who maintain this beautiful park.*

74. PACKWOOD HOUSE, HOCKLEY HEATH, WARWICKSHIRE, ENG-
LAND. *This fine old stone urn flanked by English lavender is only one of
the beautiful ornaments in this old walled garden.*

75. *GREAT FOSTERS HOTEL, EGHAM, SURREY, ENGLAND. A bronze statue of a little old-fashioned girl is the central figure in this hedged-in garden of gay snapdragons.*

76. *EASTLANDS, WEYBRIDGE, SURREY, ENGLAND.* An ancient Etrus-
can vase, which the Warwick Deepings brought back from Italy for their
garden. It is surrounded by phlox in different colors, and tall yellow achillea.

77. MT. STEWART, NEWTOWNARDS, COUNTY DOWN, NORTH-
ERN IRELAND. *Some of the whimsical stone sculptures designed by the
Marchioness of Londonderry for her garden. There is a Dodo bird on top
of a Noah's Ark, and rabbits, greyhounds, and a small prehistoric monster.*

78. *POWERSCOURT, ENNISKERRY, COUNTY WICKLOW, EIRE. One of the many authentic Italian sculptures stands at the entrance to the terraced slope.*

79. *POWERSCOURT, ENNISKERRY, COUNTY WICKLOW, EIRE. The bluish patina on this fine Italian bronze urn is an integral part of the misty blue mountains beyond.*

80. HERRENHAUSEN, HANNOVER, GERMANY. *The open-air stage is enclosed by tall hedges forming "wings," which were planted toward the end of the 17th century. Against this dark background gilded Dutch statues are placed. There are seats for 800 people, and concerts, plays, and ballets are given here regularly throughout the summer.*

81. *WESTBROEK PARK, THE HAGUE, HOLLAND.* *An amusing sand-stone statue by A. C. Roth, of two ladies under an umbrella, holding a small dog.*

82. ZAANSE SCHANS, ZAANDAM, HOLLAND. *This gay little stone figure of the period adds much to the charm of this private garden restored in the 18th-century manner.*

83. BAGATELLE, PARIS, FRANCE. The white statue is set off in dramatic contrast against an old Cedar of Lebanon in this lovely rose garden.

84. *CHÂTEAU DE VERSAILLES, FRANCE. One of the most beautiful of the many urns decorating the railings and posts of this great garden. It is of blue-green bronze.*

85. *CHÂTEAU DE VERSAILLES, FRANCE. An exquisite white urn decorating the garden, with a view of the great pool beyond.*

86. *VILLA I TATTI, SETTIGNANO, ITALY. This statue has a large bed of
marigolds as background, and is framed by lemon trees in terra-cotta pots.*

87. *VILLA I TATTI, SETTIGNANO, ITALY. The white statues are carefully placed in front of dark shrubs for effect. The background of the deep yellow villa with blue-green door and shutters adds warmth to the scene.*

88. *VILLA GARZONI, COLLODI, ITALY. This elaborate staircase ornamented with statuary and balustrades is typical of Italian gardens of the 17th century.*

89. *LA MORTOLA, VILLA HANBURY, VENTIMIGLIA, ITALY. The little white pavilion has a domed roof of delicately designed ironwork.*

90. *MARIMURTRA, BLANES, SPAIN. The small temple is framed by dark cypresses and a rocky peak, with a view of the blue Mediterranean beyond.*

91. *PACKWOOD HOUSE, HOCKLEY HEATH, WARWICKSHIRE, ENG-*
LAND. This amazing row of clipped yews is 25 feet high and over 300
years old. They represent Christ's disciples and the multitude listening to the
Sermon on the Mount.

92. *GREAT DIXTER, NORTHIAM, SUSSEX, ENGLAND.* The *topiary peacocks of yew in this fine garden are famous.*

93. HIDCOTE MANOR, CHIPPING CAMPDEN, GLOUCESTERSHIRE, ENGLAND. *Two topiary birds frame in the fuchsia garden entrance and the fountain pool. The arched pediment doorway at the rear is also of clipped yew.*

94. HASELEY COURT, LITTLE HASELEY, OXFORDSHIRE, ENGLAND.
One can easily distinguish the knights, castles, pawns, and so on, of one of the finest sets of topiary chessmen in England, because they are so well arranged and the boxwood and yew so well cut.

95. *HEVER CASTLE, EDENBRIDGE, KENT, ENGLAND. Another set of topiary chessmen of golden yew, planted in the 20th century but in the period style of the castle. There is a rose garden in front.*

96. *AVEBURY MANOR, MARLBOROUGH, WILTSHIRE, ENGLAND.*
Beautifully clipped topiaries separate beds of English lavender.

97. *AVEBURY MANOR, MARLBOROUGH, WILTSHIRE, ENGLAND.*
The famous old topiary garden in front of the 16th-century manor house.

98. GREAT FOSTERS HOTEL, EGHAM, SURREY, ENGLAND. The yew topiary bird on its nest looks out over formal garden beds filled with ageratum and marigolds.

99. THE PRIORY, HURLEY, BERKSHIRE, ENGLAND. *A wonderful example of the corkscrew topiary form, seen from inside the house.*

100. EASTLANDS, WEYBRIDGE, SURREY, ENGLAND. *An excellent use of low topiaries carefully placed to accent the design of the flower garden.*

101. *MT. STEWART, NEWTOWNARDS, COUNTY DOWN, NORTH-*
ERN IRELAND. Clipped yew arches form the background of this sunken
Spanish Garden.

102. *MT. STEWART, NEWTOWNARDS, COUNTY DOWN, NORTH-
ERN IRELAND. In this garden full of delightfully witty statuary and
topiary forms, perhaps the most charming is this procession cut on top of
a hedge.*

103. *EARLSHALL, LEUCHARS, FIFE, SCOTLAND. Imaginative yew to-piaries in front of the beautiful restored 16th-century castle.*

104. EARLSHALL, LEUCHARS, FIFE, SCOTLAND. *This grouping of old yew topiaries represents chessmen.*

105. *KINROSS HOUSE KINROSS, KINROSS-SHIRE, SCOTLAND. The corkscrew shape is a great favorite among topiary artists. A pole is set close to the trunk when it is first planted, and the branches are wound around it and clipped as the shrub grows.*

106. POWIS CASTLE, WELSHPOOL, MONTGOMERYSHIRE, WALES.
Some of the yews here are 200 years old. The one on the left of this terrace walk has been cut into mushroom shape as a summer house to contain a bench.

107. CHIRK CASTLE, DENBIGHSHIRE, WALES. *A close view of some of the extraordinary topiaries, several hundred years old, and one of the lovely gates of the castle.*

108. *GWYDYR CASTLE, LLANWRST, DENBIGHSHIRE, WALES. The huge low lines of topiaries frame the misty mountains in the distance, as well as serving as a dignified stage setting for a peacock.*

109. *KASTEEL TWICKEL, DELDEN, HOLLAND. One of the most charming topiaries in the French Garden represents a bird sitting on a nest close to the castle moat.*

110. *VILLA LA PIETRA, FLORENCE, ITALY. These topiaries seem to suggest baskets or even cardinals' mitres.*

111. GENERALIFE, GRANADA, SPAIN. *A walk lined with potted plants leads through clipped yew arches to the gardens beyond.*

28C. NYMANS GARDENS, HANDCROSS, SUSSEX, ENGLAND. *This fine yew specimen of topiary art has been cut as an open-work finial on a pedestal. Orange montbretias make a gay bouquet at its base.*

29C. HERRENHAUSEN, HANOVER, GERMANY. *In one of the "Secret Gardens" behind tall hedges is a charming array of small topiary animals placed among low flowers in pleasing color schemes.*

6

WATER IN THE GARDEN

A.   Streams

30C. ETTLINGEN, GERMANY. *A canal bridge leading to the Town Hall is gaily decorated with geraniums and petunias.*

112. MT. USHER, ASHFORD, COUNTY WICKLOW, EIRE. *The river flowing through this botanical paradise is planted along its banks with azaleas, pampas-grass, and other fine specimens, always keeping a completely natural look. Small waterfalls and bridges interrupt its course at intervals.*

113. *MT. USHER, ASHFORD, COUNTY WICKLOW, EIRE. An unusually decorative way to use a white clematis, as a border along the stream.*

172

114. ANNESGROVE, CASTLETOWNROCHE, COUNTY CORK, EIRE.
At one of the little waterfalls of the River Awbeg stands a Gunnera mani-
cata. *When full grown, the leaves often stretch six feet across. Even this
young specimen has a huge pine-cone-like inflorescence. Flowering cherries
arch overhead.*

115. CRARAE LODGE, MINARD, ARGYLL, SCOTLAND. *In a typical small highland glen beside the stream, fine hybrid rhododendrons and azaleas have been planted in a seemingly natural manner.*

116. *TIVOLI GARDENS, COPENHAGEN, DENMARK. A unique fountain enclosed in glass tubes. Watching the bubbles constantly rising inside and catching the sunlight or artificial night lighting, one is almost mesmerized by their beauty. Each column is topped by a gilded crown or other ornament.*

117. *TIVOLI GARDENS, COPENHAGEN, DENMARK. An amusing life-
sized lady of blue-and-white Copenhagen porcelain holds an urn on her
head from which spouts a fountain, while other streams spurt from her
arms.*

118. *CHÂTEAU VAUX-LE-VICOMTE, MAINCY, FRANCE. One of the large round pools with fountains, surrounded by occasional statues and conical yews.*

119. KURPARK, BADEN-BADEN, GERMANY. *A typical two-tiered ba-roque fountain with a sculptured figure kneeling in front. Urns filled with geraniums decorate the steps leading to a terrace.*

120. *WESTFALENPARK, DORTMUND, GERMANY. One of the great attractions in this flower-filled park is the "Water Organ." On weekends and many evenings the fountains' sprays are "played" in synchronized rhythm to the music of a great organ, the waters rising and falling, soaring or lightly dancing to fit the classical symphonies.*

121. NORDPARK, DUESSELDORF, GERMANY. Near the entrance of this beautiful park lies a long rectangular pool, across which arch many small sprays in the Spanish manner. Occasionally a short perpendicular fountain adds to the pattern.

122. VILLA LANTE DI BAGNAIA, VITERBO, ITALY. At the entrance to this 16th-century estate lies this large pool with a black horse as its central fountain. Other sculptures surround it, both in the water and on the high curved wall above.

123. VILLA D'ESTE, TIVOLI, ITALY. The most dramatic of all the fountain groups in this garden. Ten smaller fountains rise from an upper terrace, while two very large ones frame the waterfall and round fountain below. All are reflected in the great pool.

124. VILLA D'ESTE, TIVOLI, ITALY. *A closer look at the combination of
fountains and waterfalls just below the first terrace.*

125. VILLA D'ESTE, TIVOLI, ITALY. The famous long wall of 100 small fountains, each coming from a different sculpture with others lined up above. All the stonework is covered with exquisite mosses and tiny ferns.

126. *VILLA D'ESTE, TIVOLI, ITALY. Visitors enjoy going into the back entrance of this fountain and walking about under the showers of water.*

31C. TIVOLI GARDENS, COPENHAGEN, DENMARK. *A series of small fountains in one of the garden restaurants, surrounded by roses and delphiniums.*

32C. *VILLA CARLOTTA, CADENABBIA, LAKE COMO, ITALY.* This *beautifully shaped pool is surrounded by small beds of begonias and potted juniper trees.*

33C. *MUSÉE ÎLE-DE-FRANCE, St. JEAN-CAP-FERRAT, FRANCE.* The *Spanish Garden with its long pool rimmed with salvia and red-leaved* Amaranthus.

127. GREAT DIXTER, NORTHIAM, SUSSEX, ENGLAND. *The pool in this sunken garden is surrounded by flagstones and walls furry with small herbs and rock plants.*

128. BLENHEIM PALACE, WOODSTOCK, OXFORDSHIRE, ENGLAND.
*Called the "English Versailles," the garden has a very beautiful succession
of pools draining into each other with tiny waterfalls. They are surrounded
by scalloped parterres of boxwood and crushed brick, and smaller pools.*

129. SYON PARK GARDENING CENTRE, BRENTFORD, MIDDLE-
SEX, ENGLAND. *One of the features of the demonstration electric
garden is this electrically run waterfall. A rock garden surrounds the pool.*

130. HERRENHAUSEN, HANNOVER, GERMANY. *Another of the "Secret Gardens," here surrounded by a tall hedge just as it was in the 17th century. It is planted on an island surrounded by water and small fountains. The center is a beautifully scrolled boxwood parterre in white gravel. Around this are old urns and statues and great pots of blue Lily-of-the-Nile (Agapanthus umbellatus).*

131. *VILLA GARZONI, COLLODI, ITALY. A large round basin makes a quiet spot below the very elaborate flowerbeds on the hillside.*

193

132. *VILLA GAMBERAIA, SETTIGNANO, ITALY. One of the rectangular pools reflects the charming cream-colored villa, the clipped topiary shrubs, and occasional accents of red geraniums.*

133. *VILLA GAMBERAIA, SETTIGNANO, ITALY. A corner of one of the pools, showing the stone ornaments and rounded yews.*

134. *ALHAMBRA, GRANADA, SPAIN. The shape of this small waterlily pool is particularly lovely.*

135. *ALHAMBRA, GRANADA, SPAIN. Typical of the planning of the gardens at this ancient Moorish pleasure palace, the long pool makes a peaceful picture with its reflections of the exquisite columns, arches, and the massive tower.*

136. *QUINTA DE MARQUEZ DE FRONTEIRA, BEMFICA, PORTUGAL.*
A scrolled baroque pool in the Jardim de Benus lies in front of a delicately ornamented pavilion.